NOAH
and the People of Faith

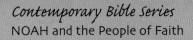

Contemporary Bible Series
NOAH and the People of Faith

Retold by Joy Melissa Jensen

Published by Scandinavia Publishing House 2009
Drejervej 15,3   DK-2400 Copenhagen NV, Denmark
Tel. (45) 3531 0330 Fax (45) 3536 0334
E-mail: info@scanpublishing.dk
Web: www.scanpublishing.dk

NOAH

and the People of Faith

Retold for Children

by Joy Melissa Jensen

scandinavia

Contents

God Makes Heaven and Earth

Genesis 1:1-19

In the beginning, God created heaven and earth. The earth was a dark and empty place. There was only a roaring black ocean covering empty land. The Spirit of God called out in the darkness, "Let there be light!" Suddenly light shone down and created the first day.

On the second day, God said, "Let the sky be separated from the ocean, and let the ocean be separated from the dry land." The ocean, the land and the sky all obeyed God's command.

On the third day, God said, "Let there be plants and trees so that the earth may be filled with living things." The earth obeyed. Trees spread their big leafy branches, and little flowers and plants sprung up out of the ground to greet the sun.

On the fourth day, God said, "Let the moon and stars shine at night, and let the sun shine by day. These lights will mark the seasons and shed light on the earth." God looked around and saw that all that He had done was good.

4

God Makes the Creatures of the Ocean and the Sky

Genesis 1:20-25; 2:3-6

On the fifth day, God said, "Let the ocean be filled with sea creatures!" Just then, the water began to churn with life. Great whales lifted their mighty heads. Dolphins jumped and splashed in the sunlight and little sea crabs scuttled along the sea floor.

God saw all this was good, so He said, "Let the sky be filled with creatures of the air!" Seagulls swooped in the breeze along with butterflies and buzzing insects. God created all of them, big and small, and to each He gave His blessing.

God Makes
the Animals of the Earth

Genesis 1:20-25; 2:3-6

God was happy with the creatures of the sea and the air. "Now for the dry land," God said, "Let the deserts and valleys and mountains be filled with animals!" And that's what happened. Elephants trumpeted loudly, giraffes stretched out their spotted necks toward the trees and porcupines waddled on the ground with their prickly bodies. The earth was home to animals of all shapes and sizes, both wild and tame. God loved watching them play with each other. He was very pleased and blessed each and every one of them.

9

God Makes the First People

Genesis 1:26-27; 2:7, Genesis 18-25, 1:28-2:3

On the sixth day God looked around at all the animals of the earth, and the animals of the sea and sky. Still God felt lonely. Something was missing. So God said, "I will create man. He will be special because I will make him in my image."

Then God took a handful of soil and out of it he made Adam. God loved Adam. He even let Adam name all the animals. But God said, "It isn't good for man to be alone."

So God took Adam's rib while he was asleep, and out of it He created the first woman. Her name was Eve. She was the perfect partner for Adam, and Adam loved her.

God gave Adam and Eve His blessing. He said, "The earth is filled with animals you may rule over, and many good plants and fruits you may eat. Fill the earth with your children, and care for all the living creatures!"

God was exhausted from all His hard work so He created the seventh day as a special day of rest.

The Garden of Eden

Genesis 2:8-17

God put Adam and Eve in a garden called Eden. The Garden of Eden was a lush and colorful paradise. Plump ripe fruit grew from the trees, flowers blossomed and waterfalls crashed down merrily with clear, cool water.

In the middle of the garden, God placed a tree called the tree of knowledge. The fruit eaten from this tree gave the power to know the difference between right and wrong. God told Adam and Eve that they could eat from any of the trees in the garden, except for the fruit from the tree of knowledge. "If you eat from that tree," God warned, "you can no longer live in the garden."

Adam and Eve Disobey God

Genesis 3:1-7

One day a snake slithered up to Eve as she was walking in the garden. He hissed at her. "Eve," he said, "Why don't you take a bite from that juicy piece of fruit hanging from the tree of knowledge?" Eve remembered what God had said. "God told us we must not eat fruit from that tree," she replied. To this, the snake answered, "That is only because the fruit will allow you to know the difference between right and wrong. God doesn't want you to be as wise as Him."

The snake made Eve curious. "What would be the harm in one tiny bite?" Eve said to herself. So she sunk her teeth into the fruit and tasted it. Then Eve handed the fruit to Adam and he also took a bite. For the first time, Adam and Eve looked at each other and realized they were both naked. They were embarrassed and quickly covered them-selves up with the biggest fig leaves they could find.

14

Out of Eden

Genesis 3:20-23

That afternoon, Adam and Eve heard God walking in the Garden of Eden. They were frightened because they knew they had disobeyed Him. They hid behind the trees and plants, hoping God would not discover what they had done. But God knows all things.   God called out to Adam, "Why did you disobey what I said and eat the fruit from the tree of knowledge?"

Adam answered, "Eve was the one who took the fruit. It's her fault!" And Eve said, "But it was the snake who told me to take the fruit. So it's the snake's fault!"

God loved Adam and Eve very much. He was disappointed that they did not listen to His command but chose to listen to the sneaky snake instead. He gave Adam and Eve some animal skins to cover themselves up from the cold. Then He cast them out of the Garden of Eden. They had to live on dry land and work hard for their food.

Cain and Abel

Genesis 4:1-5

Adam and Eve had two sons. The older son was named Cain. He farmed the land. The younger son, Abel, was a sheep farmer.

One time when the brothers were still young men, they made an offering to show God how much they loved Him.

Cain saved part of his harvest grain and offered it to God. Abel killed the firstborn lamb from one of the sheep. He butchered the lamb, cut off the best parts and offered them to God. God was pleased. He accepted Abel's offering, but He didn't accept Cain's offering.

Cain was filled with jealousy toward his brother Abel. So God said to Cain, "Why are you upset? If you do what is right I will accept your offering!" But Cain wasn't listening. He was too busy trying to figure out a way he could get back at his brother.

Cain Kills His Brother

Genesis 4:6-16

A few days later Cain said to his brother Abel, "Let's go for a walk." Abel followed his brother far off into the fields and over the rocks. When Cain was certain that they were all alone, he picked up a rock and hit Abel over the head with it.

Later that day God called out to Cain, "Where is Abel?"

Cain answered, "How should I know? Am I supposed to look after my brother?" But Cain could not fool God. "Why have you done this terrible thing?" God asked him. "You've killed your own brother. From now on you will be without a home."

So Cain had to leave his family. He wandered around from place to place, never really belonging anywhere.

Noah Builds an Ark

Genesis 6:5-22

The world God made quickly filled with more and more people. God saw all their bad deeds. They cheated, and stole and lied. God was disappointed in their behavior. He was sorry He had made them. So He decided to start over.

God planned a great flood. He would let rain pour down until it drenched the land and drowned the people. But there was one man God was pleased with. This man was good and kind-hearted. His name was Noah.

God told Noah about His plan to flood the earth. "You have made me happy," God said to Noah. "Because of that, I will save your family from the flood." Then God told Noah to gather up the thickest, strongest lumber he could find. He wanted Noah to build a boat, called an ark. God said, "Make it big enough to hold your family, and big enough to hold one male and one female of every kind of animal on earth."

Noah did just as God asked. He worked all day and all night, hammering wood planks together and building the biggest boat the world had ever seen.

The Great Flood
Genesis 7:1, 10, 13-16

Seven days later the ark was finally finished. Noah made sure to have a special place ready for each kind of animal. He packed the ark full of food and supplies. Then the rain began—first a pitter-patter, and then a torrent. The dry land was covered in water. Noah knew the time had come for God's great flood.

Noah went into the ark with his wife and children. Then the animals marched inside. Two by two, the animals crawled into their stalls. Everyone was glad to be safe on Noah's ark. Noah made sure his family was on board. Then he counted all the animals. Yep, Everyone was there. They were ready to go! The flood rose higher, and God closed the door to the ark.

Forty Days and Forty Nights of Rain

Genesis 7:17-24, Genesis 8 1-19

Rain poured down for forty days and forty nights. The flood was so deep that it covered the highest mountain peaks! Nothing on earth survived. Only Adam, his family and the animals were saved. God was watching over them.

When it stopped raining, Noah sent out a raven in search of land. The raven came back, unable to find a place of dry land anywhere. So Noah sent out a dove. The dove returned, just like the raven. But when Noah sent the dove out a second time, it returned with a branch from an olive tree. The bird had found land! Then Noah sent out the dove one last time. But this time the dove never returned.

"I have ended the flood," God said to Noah, "You can leave the ark now." So Noah opened the door and called everybody out of the boat. Each of God's animals stepped off the boat, stretching their legs, and sniffing the clean fresh air. It felt good to walk on dry land after so many days on the swaying, shaky sea.

The Rainbow's Promise

Genesis 9:1-16

God gave a blessing to Noah and his sons. He said to them, "May you have many children and grandchildren! This will be the land I will give to your families for generations to come. I saved you from the flood because you have been faithful and obeyed my commands. Now I will make a promise I will keep forever. I will never send another flood to destroy the earth again."

Just then, the sun broke through the rain clouds. A beautiful rainbow full of bright colors shone in the sky. God said, "The rainbow will be my sign to you that I always keep my promises. Every time you see a rainbow, remember I am with you. I will never leave you again."

28

The Tower of Babel

Genesis 10:32-11:4, Genesis 11:5-9

Noah's sons, Shem, Ham and Japheth had children. And their children had children too. Soon the world was filled with people again. Some of them settled in a place called Babel. The people in Babel decided to build a tower so high that it would reach heaven. "We will be famous, and God will be pleased with us!" they said to one another.

But when God saw the tall tower, He was not pleased. He saw that the people of Babel were no longer humble servants.

Instead, they were proud— believing they could reach God with their high tower. He punished the people by giving them each their own language. No one could understand each other anymore because all the languages created a confusing babble of sounds! The tower could no longer be finished. They were too busy arguing in all their different languages.

God Chooses Abram

Genesis 12:1-9, Genesis 15:1-7; 17:4-5

Abram was one of God's special people. He lived in the city of Haran. One day God said to Abram, "Leave the place that you come from, and go to the land I will show you." Abram trusted God with his whole heart. He loaded his camels with all his belongings, and left home with his wife, Sarah, and his nephew, Lot, and all their servants. They traveled through the desert hills with only God as their guide.

When Abram and his family

came to the land of Canaan, God said, "This land is yours! It will belong to your family forever. I will bless you and all the people in your family that come after you. Everyone on earth will be blessed by your life!" Abram felt very thankful so he set up an altar in the desert where he could worship God. Then Abram and the rest of his group journeyed onward. Finally they came to a place they liked and pitched their tents and settled.

The Promise of God

Genesis 18:1-15

Abram was growing older. God had given him many things—a good wife, land and animals. But there was one thing Abram wanted that God had not given him. Abram wanted to have a child with his wife Sarah. They had tried to have a child before, but God had never blessed them with one. Now they had wrinkles and gray hair. They had given up hope of ever being parents.

One evening God said to Abram, "Your name will be changed to Abraham because you will be the father of many nations. Look at all the brilliant night sky! Can you count the stars? That is how many descendents you will have!" Abraham said, "I trust you God! You have already given me everything I could ask for. But how can I be the father of many when I have no children?" God answered, "You will have a son with your wife Sarah. And everything you have will be his." Abraham could hardly believe it. But he had faith. He got down on his knees and thanked God.

Three Travelers

Genesis 18:20-26

One hot summer afternoon, Abraham was sitting outside his tent when three travelers came by. Abraham saw them and he jumped up and called out to them, "Come, let me get you some water to wash your tired feet!" Then Abraham ran back to the tent. "Sarah!" he said, "Would you make some bread for our guests?" Sarah got cooking while Abraham went out in search of his best calf to serve with some milk and yogurt. The men gathered around under the shady trees sharing a drink and talking. Sarah was listening by the tent door.

One of the men said, "Abraham, your wife will give birth to a son soon." When Sarah heard this, she laughed to herself. "Why did Sarah laugh?"

God asked Abraham. "Doesn't she think she can have a child in her old age? I am God and nothing is too difficult for me! I promise by this time next year you will already have your baby boy."

Good People in a Wicked City

Genesis 18:20-26

The three travelers got up to leave. Abraham walked with them a ways. God said to Abraham, "I have heard that the people of Sodom and Gomorrah are doing all kinds of evil things. I have heard that many of them sin and carry out wicked deeds. I am going to see if all of this is true. What do you think, Abraham?" Abraham thought about it. Then he turned to God and said, "What if there are fifty good people living in Sodom? Are you going to destroy those in the city who are righteous?" God answered, "I will save the city for fifty good people." Then Abraham asked, "What if there are forty good people?" And God told Abraham, "If there are forty good people, I still won't destroy the city."

Abraham thought for a moment. Then he said, "God— what about twenty good people? Will you destroy the city if there are twenty good people?" God told Abraham "If there are twenty good people, I still won't destroy the city." But Abraham was still not satisfied. "And what if there are only ten good people?" Yet again God told Abraham, "If there are only ten good people, I won't destroy the city."

Then God went on his journey toward Sodom and Gomorrah, and Abraham turned back to his tent where Sarah was waiting.

39

God Saves Lot and his Family

Genesis 19:1-29

Noah's nephew, Lot, lived in the city of Sodom. Two angels came to warn Lot of God's plan to destroy the city. Lot invited them into his home for the night. The angels told Lot, "God has plans to destroy the city of Sodom because it is turning into a dark and evil place. Your family has been faithful and good. You will be saved by God's grace."

A group of men from Sodom had gathered outside Lot's home to attack the two angels. The angels bolted the door and said, "Lot, take your family and all your relatives and leave now. God plans to burn this wicked city! Quick, leave before the city turns to ash!" Lot bundled up his family in cloaks to protect them from the sooty ash. They hurried and stumbled over the rocks and escaped from the burning city. God had not forgotten his promise to Abraham. He saved Lot and his family.

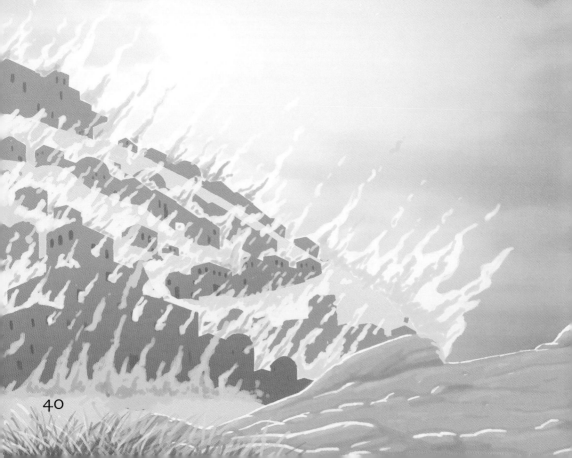

Isaac Is Born

Genesis 21:1-7

God kept His promise to Abraham and Sarah. He gave them a healthy baby boy. They named him Isaac. Isaac was a beautiful baby. Abraham was very proud. Sarah looked up at her husband and said, "Who would have guessed that we would have a son in our old age? I will never laugh at God's promises again. Now I think it's silly I ever doubted God at all!" Isaac was a good baby, and they both loved him dearly.

As Isaac grew older, Abraham and Sarah spent a lot of time with him. Abraham taught Isaac all about God's wonderful world. Sarah went on long walks with the young boy. She pointed out the animals and plants and taught Isaac their names. Abraham and Sarah knew Isaac would grow up into a strong servant of God.

Abraham Obeys God

Genesis 22:1-13, 15-18

After several years had passed, God decided to test Abraham's trust and obedience. God said to Abraham, "Go get Isaac, your son whom you love so dearly. Take him to the high mountaintop of Moriah and kill him on an altar as a sacrifice in honor of me."

Abraham's heart nearly broke with sadness when he heard God's words. Isaac was the only child he ever had; he had cared for Isaac, played with Isaac, and taught him all kinds of things. Now God was asking him to sacrifice his only child! But Abraham was filled with faith and love for God. He knew that his only choice was to obey.

Abraham got up early the next morning and chopped wood for the altar. He tied the wood into bundles. Then he told Isaac to come with him up the steep mountain.

Abraham Proves His Faith

Genesis 22:3-18

Abraham and Isaac were out of breath by the time they reached the top. Abraham took the wood and coals and made an altar in the spot where God had told him to sacrifice Isaac. Then Isaac said, "Father, we have the coals and the wood, but where is the lamb for the sacrifice?" Abraham answered sadly, "God will provide the lamb, son." Abraham knew that God had intended Isaac to be the sacrifice, but he just couldn't bring himself to tell his son.

Abraham tied up Isaac. But just as he was about to kill him, the voice of God called out, "Stop, Abraham! Don't kill Isaac! Now I know that you were willing to sacrifice the most precious thing that belonged to you. You trusted me and obeyed my command. Because of this, I will bless your family forever." Abraham sighed with relief. He sacrificed a ram to God instead. Then Abraham and Isaac went home with happy hearts, grateful to God.

A Wife for Isaac

Genesis 24:1-27

Many years went by, and Sarah had passed away. Abraham knew that soon he would be called up to heaven too. Before he died, he wanted to find a good wife for his son Isaac. Abraham called one of his most trusted servants to him. "Go to the land where I was born," Abraham told him, "My brother Nahor lives there. Find a good woman among his people for my son Isaac to marry."

When the servant arrived he was worn out from his long tiresome journey. He rested with his camels near a well. There a woman named Rebekah was filling her water jar. The servant asked her for a drink. "I'll be glad to give you a drink."

she answered. Then she saw the servant's thirsty camels and kindly offered them some water as well. Abraham's servant had brought along some gold bracelets to give as gifts, and he placed them on Rebekah's arm. "Thank you for your kindness," He told her. Then he said, "Tell me, who is your family?" Rebekah replied, "My father is Bethual, the son of Milcah and Nahor."

Abraham's servant knew that he had found the right woman for Isaac. Not only was Rebekah kind and generous, she was also Abraham's relative. The servant told Rebekah that he had come on behalf of her uncle Abraham. So she invited him back to her home to stay with her family.

49

Isaac and Rebekah

Genesis 24:28-67

Abraham's servant told Rebekah's father why he had come. "I have been sent to find a wife for my master Abraham's son, Isaac, among his relatives." Then the servant said, "Rebekah has impressed me with her gentle kindness. I would like her to come back with me and be Isaac's wife!" Rebekah's brother and father knew that this was God's plan. They were sad to see Rebekah go, but they were happy for her also.

Isaac was walking out in his father's field when the servant and Rebekah approached on their camels. Rebekah spotted Isaac right away. There was something special about him. "Who is that man walking out there?" Rebekah asked. The servant replied, "That's Isaac— the man you will marry!" So Isaac and Rebekah were married. They loved each other dearly, and Abraham could die happily knowing that Isaac had a family of his own.

Esau and Jacob

Genesis 25:19-26

Rebekah and Isaac wanted to have children, but God did not give them any. Isaac prayed to God to bring them a child. Finally God answered his prayer. Rebekah became pregnant. She knew that she was pregnant with twins because she could feel them fighting with each other inside of her!

One day God came to Rebekah and said, "You will be blessed with two boys. But just like they are fighting inside of your womb, they will fight as they grow older too. They will separate into two different nations. The younger son will be strong and great. The older son will be his servant."

After nine long months of carrying the babies inside of her, Rebekah gave birth. The first baby came out and he was covered with bright red hair! They named him Esau. The second baby came out just behind, holding onto his brothers heel. They named him Jacob.

Esau Makes a Promise

Genesis 25:27-34

Jacob and Esau were very different. Esau was an excellent hunter, while Jacob tended sheep. Esau was his father's favorite son, while Jacob was his mother's favorite son. Because Esau was the oldest, he had certain birthrights that Jacob did not have.

One evening, Jacob was cooking a stew at his camp. Esau was out on a hunt when he smelled the delicious food wafting up from the pot. "That red stew you're cooking smells good, brother. May I have some?" Esau asked. "Yes," Jacob said, "I will give you some of my stew if you promise to give me something in return."

"What do you want?" asked Esau who was growing hungrier by the minute, and was happy to agree to anything. "Sell me your birthrights," replied Jacob. Esau quickly reached for the bowl of stew. "Sure, why not?" Esau said without a thought, "What good are they to me, anyway?" Then he gulped down the soup, while Jacob smiled to himself. He knew that he had tricked his brother.

54

Isaac Blesses Jacob

Genesis 27:1-40

Isaac was now old and blind and close to dying. Before he died, he wanted to give his oldest son, Esau, a special blessing. It was his birthright as the eldest son. Because Rebekah loved Jacob the best, she wanted Jacob to have the blessing instead of his brother.

"Go to your father," Rebekah said to Jacob one evening, "He will think you are your brother Esau, and he will give you his blessing!" But Jacob said, "My brother is a hairy man, and I am not. If my father finds out I am tricking him, he will curse me!" Rebekah was a clever woman. She quickly took some goatskins and wrapped them around Jacob's arms.

Then Jacob went to his father and said, "It's me, Esau." Isaac reached out and felt his hairy arms, and believed that he was telling the truth. He laid his hands on his son's head and gave a blessing that endowed him with strength, and courage. This blessing meant that God would be with him forever.

When Esau came home he rushed in to see his father. "Father, it's Esau—I'm home from my hunt, and I've brought you some meat!" Isaac suddenly realized he had given his blessing to the wrong son! Esau and his father were upset, but it was already too late. Jacob had God's blessing.

Rebekah Sends Jacob Away

Genesis 27:41-45

Esau was furious at his brother Jacob for tricking him. He had forgotten about the promise he had made to Jacob to give him his birthrights. He thought Jacob had unrightfully stolen his blessing. He boiled inside with anger toward Jacob. He decided that after his father died, he would kill Jacob.

When Rebekah found out what Esau planned to do, she ran to Jacob. "Jacob, my son!" she cried, "Your brother Esau is angrier with you than he's ever been! He is just waiting for the time when he can kill you! Listen carefully and do what I say. Go to the home of my brother Laban in the town of Haran and stay with him for a while. When it is safe, I'll send for you to come home again."

Jacob packed his things and prepared to leave his family home. Rebekah sent Jacob off on his long journey with a mournful wave goodbye. She was sorry to see her beloved son leave.

Jacob's Dream

Genesis 28: 10-22

Jacob traveled over hot deserts and dry plains. He was worn out and stopped just before nightfall to find a good place to sleep. After he found a good spot, he lay down and rested his head on a rock for a pillow.

That night Jacob had a brilliant dream. He saw a ladder that reached from the ground up to heaven. God's angels were going up and down the ladder.

God spoke to him and said, "Jacob, I have been with your father, and your grandfather. Now I am with you. I will give you and your family the land on which you are now sleeping. Your descendents will be as many as the specks of dust on the ground! I will never leave you or the people that come after you!"

Jacob woke up early the next morning feeling rested and peaceful. He remembered his dream. Then he stood the rock he had used as a pillow on its end. He poured olive oil on the rock in honor of God. Then Jacob kneeled down and prayed, "Watch over me Lord God, and I will worship you forever."

The Contemporary Bible Series